NFL's TOP 10
GAMES

by Brian Howell

NFL's
TOP TEN

SportsZone

An Imprint of Abdo Publishing
abdopublishing.com

abdopublishing.com

Published by Abdo Publishing, a division of ABDO, PO Box 398166, Minneapolis, Minnesota 55439. Copyright © 2018 by Abdo Consulting Group, Inc. International copyrights reserved in all countries. No part of this book may be reproduced in any form without written permission from the publisher. SportsZone™ is a trademark and logo of Abdo Publishing.

Printed in the United States of America, North Mankato, Minnesota
052017
092017

THIS BOOK CONTAINS
RECYCLED MATERIALS

Cover Photo: Mark J. Terrill/AP Images
Interior Photos: Perry Knotts/AP Images, 4–5; Rich Clarkson/Sports Illustrated/Getty Images, 7; Al Messerschmidt/AP Images, 9; Al Golub/AP Images, 10–11; Ed Reinke/AP Images, 13; Amy Sancetta/AP Images, 12–13; Scott Boehm/AP Images, 15; Peter Read Miller/AP Images, 16; Matt Rourke/AP Images, 17; Matt Slocum/AP Images, 19; Stephan Savoia/AP Images, 18–19; Tony Tomsic/AP Images, 21; AP Images, 22, 23; Hy Peskin/Sports Illustrated/Getty Images, 24, 25; Robert Riger/Hulton Archive/Getty Images, 26; Robert Riger/Getty Images Sport/Getty Images, 27

Editor: Patrick Donnelly
Series Designer: Craig Hinton

Publisher's Cataloging-in-Publication Data

Names: Howell, Brian, author.
Title: NFL's top 10 games / by Brian Howell.
Other titles: NFL's top ten games
Description: Minneapolis, MN : Abdo Publishing, 2018. | Series: NFL's top ten | Includes bibliographical references and index.
Identifiers: LCCN 2016963092 | ISBN 9781532111402 (lib. bdg.) | ISBN 9781680789256 (ebook)
Subjects: LCSH: National Football League--Juvenile literature. | Football----United States--History--Juvenile literature. | Football--United States--Miscellanea--Juvenile literature. | Football--United States--Statistics--Juvenile literature.
Classification: DDC 796.332--dc23
LC record available at http://lccn.loc.gov/2016963092

Table of
CONTENTS

Introduction

The National Football League (NFL) began play in 1920. Its teams have played thousands of games. Hundreds of them have been played for championships. Countless games have come down to the final seconds.

So what makes a game one of the best ever?

The greatest games usually have something big on the line. They often feature legendary players, remarkable plays, or thrilling finishes. And some games have a long-lasting impact on the sport.

Read on to learn more about the best games in NFL history.

10

Garo Yepremian, *far left*, was the hero of the day for Miami after making the game-winning field goal.

Christmas Dinner Delayed

On Christmas Day in 1971, NFL fans got a gift of extra football from the Miami Dolphins and Kansas City Chiefs. Squaring off in the first round of the American Football Conference (AFC) playoffs, the teams played the longest game in NFL history.

The Dolphins and Chiefs met on a muddy field in Kansas City's old Municipal Stadium. They were evenly matched with identical 10–3–1 records. Each team's offense ranked in the NFL's top 10, and both defenses were among the top five in the league. So it was no surprise when they were tied 10–10 at halftime and 17–17 after three quarters.

Chiefs running back Ed Podolak had a memorable day. He rushed for 85 yards, caught 8 passes for 110 yards, and had three long kickoff returns. Podolak accounted for 350 total yards on the day, which remained an NFL playoff record through 2016. He also scored two touchdowns. Podolak's 3-yard run gave the Chiefs a 24–17 lead heading into the final minutes.

But Miami wouldn't go away. With 1 minute, 25 seconds to play, Dolphins quarterback Bob Griese threw a 5-yard touchdown pass to tight end Marv Fleming. That tied the game yet again. But Podolak returned the Dolphins' kickoff 78 yards to the Miami 22-yard line, well within the range of Hall of Fame kicker Jan Stenerud.

But it was not to be Stenerud's day. He'd already missed a 30-yard field goal in the second quarter. Then he missed again from 32 yards out with 35 seconds to play.

On the opening possession of overtime, Dolphins star linebacker Nick Buoniconti blocked Stenerud's 42-yard attempt. Miami kicker Garo Yepremian later came up short on a 52-yarder. The struggle continued into the second overtime period. Finally, bruising Miami running back Larry Csonka ripped off a 29-yard run to set up Yepremian for a 37-yard field goal to win the game 27–24.

The rivals had battled for 82 minutes and 40 seconds. In the end, the Dolphins survived, and Christmas dinner could finally be served.

9

Elway Drives Denver

John Elway specialized in carrying the Denver Broncos to victory when all hope appeared to be lost. He finished his career with 35 fourth-quarter comebacks, more than all but four quarterbacks in NFL history. His most famous rescue took place on a frigid winter day in January 1987 when the Cleveland Browns hosted the Broncos in the AFC Championship Game.

With a trip to the Super Bowl on the line, the teams matched each other move for move. Neither side led by more than seven points. The game was tied 10–10 at halftime and knotted up 13–13 early in the fourth quarter.

Then the Browns made their move. Quarterback Bernie Kosar hit wide receiver Brian Brennan for a 48-yard touchdown with 5:43 to play. Trailing 20–13 with the ball at their 2-yard line and 81,000 roaring Browns fans shaking the Municipal Stadium bleachers, Denver needed a miracle.

During the next five minutes, Elway delivered. The 26-year-old signal caller marched the Broncos 98 yards in 15 plays. He went 6-for-9 for 78 yards through the air. He also picked up a total of 20 yards on two huge scrambles.

The Broncos beat the Browns in the AFC Championship Game three times in four seasons (1986–89). But each time they were blown out in the Super Bowl. Elway finally won the big one in each of his last two NFL seasons (1997–98).

The key play in the drive came just after the 2-minute warning. Browns defensive lineman Dave Puzzuoli sacked Elway to put Denver in a big hole. On third-and-18 from the Cleveland 48, Elway fired a strike to Mark Jackson for 20 yards and a first down. Five plays later, he hit Jackson in the end zone from 5 yards out. Rich Karlis booted the extra point, and the game was tied 20–20 with 39 seconds left.

Denver won the overtime coin flip, and Elway led another big drive, this one covering 60 yards in nine plays. Karlis drilled a 33-yard field goal to send the Broncos to the Super Bowl.

8

Stretch for "The Catch"

Dwight Clark jumped as high as he could. He stretched his arms as far as possible. His long, strong fingers snatched the football out of the air. And NFL history was made.

It was in the final minute of the National Football Conference (NFC) Championship Game in January 1982. San Francisco's Candlestick Park had been witness to a great battle between "America's Team," the Dallas Cowboys, and the new kids on the block, the San Francisco 49ers.

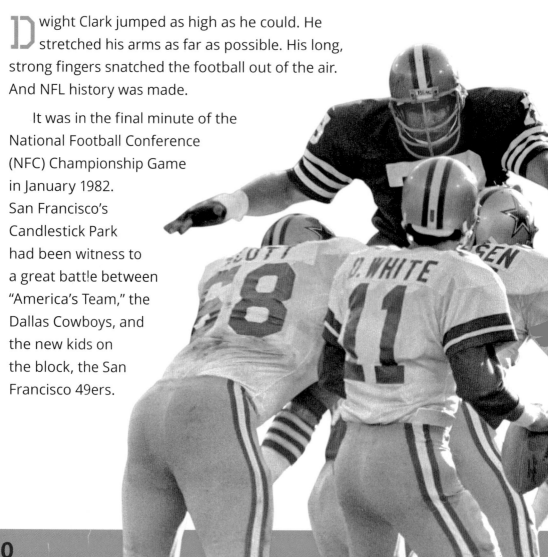

Dallas had been to the Super Bowl five times before, winning it twice. San Francisco had never been there. The closest the 49ers had come was the NFC Championship Game after the 1970 and 1971 seasons. They lost both games—to the Cowboys.

San Francisco got its chance at redemption a decade later. But with a minute to play, Dallas led 27–21. The Niners were 6 yards away from the end zone. Quarterback Joe Montana took the snap and ran to his right. Looking toward the end zone, he scrambled to the sideline and waited for a receiver to get open.

Finally, Montana floated a pass to the back of the end zone. The ball was thrown high enough that only one man could get it. The 6-foot-4-inch Clark jumped to make the grab. The play was so important that even today NFL fans still refer to it simply as "The Catch."

But the 49ers couldn't celebrate yet. Dallas trailed 28–27, but it still had a potent offense and enough time to move into field-goal range. Taking over at his 25-yard line with 47 seconds to play, quarterback Danny White immediately hit wide receiver Drew Pearson over the middle for 31 yards. Only a game-saving tackle by Niners defensive back Eric Wright kept Pearson from sprinting to the end zone.

The Cowboys needed about 15 more yards to give kicker Rafael Septien a realistic shot at a game-winning field goal. But on the next play, the San Francisco pass rush converged on White. Defensive tackle Lawrence Pillers threw him to the ground. The ball popped out, and San Francisco's Jim Stuckey recovered. The 49ers were on their way to their first Super Bowl.

7

Peyton Manning celebrates after Joseph Addai scored the go-ahead touchdown in the fourth quarter.

Colts Charge Back

Peyton Manning was hoping to put a history of playoff failure behind him. Going into the 2006 season, the Indianapolis Colts' star quarterback had a 3–6 record in the playoffs. And he'd been knocked out by Tom Brady and the New England Patriots in 2003 and 2004.

The Colts got another shot at the Patriots in the AFC Championship Game after the 2006 season. Early in the game, it didn't look like Manning's fortunes would change. New England's Asante Samuel returned an interception 39 yards for a touchdown, and the Patriots led 21–3 early in the second quarter. No team had ever trailed by that much and come back to win a conference championship game.

But the Colts were resilient. Manning ran for a touchdown and passed for another. Colts center Jeff Saturday recovered a teammate's fumble in the end zone for a touchdown early in the fourth quarter, tying the game at 28–28.

Addai played a big role in the Colts' final drive.

The Patriots eventually regained the lead 34–31 on Stephen Gostowski's 43-yard field goal with 3:49 to play. The Colts then went three-and-out and had to punt. All New England needed was a first down or two and the Patriots could run out the clock.

But the Indianapolis defense held, and a Patriots punt gave Manning one more shot. He began from his own 20-yard line with 2:17 to go. He didn't let this chance slip by. He connected with Reggie Wayne for 11 yards. He hit Bryan Fletcher for 32 more. A 14-yard connection with Wayne and a roughing-the-passer penalty put the Colts at New England's 11-yard line with 1:53 to go.

Most observers expected the Colts to keep the ball in the hands of their veteran Pro Bowl quarterback. Instead, they turned to rookie running back Joseph Addai, who barreled into the line three straight times. On third-and-2 from the Patriots 3-yard line, Addai surged into the end zone, giving the Colts their first lead of the game, 38–34.

Brady's last-gasp attempt at his own comeback was snuffed by Marlin Jackson's interception. At long last, Manning had led the Colts to the Super Bowl.

6

Santonio Holmes barely gets his toes down in the end zone as Arizona safety Aaron Francisco, *47*, tries to push him out of bounds.

Super Santonio

Only the tips of Santonio Holmes' toes touched the grass. That was enough to clinch one of the greatest Super Bowls ever.

Holmes and the Pittsburgh Steelers were facing the Arizona Cardinals in the Super Bowl after the 2008 season. The Steelers had won the Super Bowl five times, tying them with San Francisco for the most by any team. The Cardinals were in the big game for the first time.

With three minutes left, Pittsburgh held a 20–14 lead. That's when the fun really started.

The Steelers had the ball, but they were backed up at their own 1-yard line. Quarterback Ben Roethlisberger threw a pass to Holmes to get them out of trouble. But the Steelers were called for holding in the end zone on the play. The penalty resulted in a safety, giving the Cardinals two points and the ball.

Suddenly it was a 20–16 game, and Arizona had the ball at its own 36-yard line. It didn't take long for quarterback Kurt Warner to strike. He hit wide receiver Larry Fitzgerald on a short pass over the middle. Fitzgerald took it the rest of the way for a 64-yard touchdown. The Cardinals led 23–20 with 2:37 to play.

That turned out to be plenty of time for Roethlisberger. Taking over at his own 22, he completed five of six passes as the Steelers reached the

LONG HAUL FOR HARRISON

Steelers linebacker James Harrison made one of the best defensive plays in Super Bowl history against the Cardinals. As the first half was ending, he intercepted a Warner pass at his own goal line. Then he rumbled 100 yards the other way, outrunning the entire Cardinals offense for a Pittsburgh touchdown.

Arizona 6-yard line with only 43 seconds left. That's when he found his favorite target. Roethlisberger threw a laser to the back corner of the end zone just over a leaping defender. Holmes grabbed it and dragged his toes on the grass as another defender knocked him out of bounds.

The Steelers held on for a 27–23 win that gave them more Super Bowl rings than any other NFL team.

Seahawks coach Pete Carroll stares in disbelief as his offense walks off the field after Malcolm Butler's interception.

Pete's Puzzling Play Call

The Super Bowl after the 2014 season was a battle between two of the most successful teams in recent history. The New England Patriots had ruled the AFC for years. The Seattle Seahawks came into the game as the defending Super Bowl champions.

Throughout the day, the game was as close as expected.

Patriots star quarterback Tom Brady threw two early touchdown passes. Seattle's two biggest offensive stars—running back Marshawn Lynch and quarterback Russell Wilson—also produced touchdowns. The game was tied 14–14 at halftime.

A field goal early in the third quarter gave Seattle its first lead. Then Wilson hit Doug Baldwin on a short touchdown pass to put the Seahawks on top 24–14. But Brady wasn't done. He threw two touchdown passes in the game's last eight minutes to give the Patriots a 28–24 lead.

Butler falls to the ground with his game-saving interception.

HARD TO BEAT BRADY

In beating the Seahawks, Brady won his fourth Super Bowl. That tied Joe Montana (San Francisco) and Terry Bradshaw (Pittsburgh) for the most ever by a quarterback. He then broke the record two years later when the Patriots beat the Atlanta Falcons for Brady's fifth Super Bowl ring.

As great as the game was to that point, it will always be remembered for how it ended. Seattle drove to the New England 1-yard line. It was the second down with only 30 seconds to play. The Seahawks had Lynch, one of the most powerful running backs in the NFL. Most people expected him to get the ball and power his way into the end zone for the game-winning touchdown.

Instead, Seattle coach Pete Carroll called for a pass. Wilson tried to hit wide receiver Ricardo Lockette on a quick slant at the goal line. But Patriots rookie cornerback Malcolm Butler jumped in front of Lockette and intercepted the pass.

The Patriots and their fans celebrated another Super Bowl win. Seahawks fans will always wonder why their team didn't put the ball in the hands of their star running back.

4

19 and Uh-oh

The New England Patriots weren't just facing the New York Giants in the Super Bowl in February 2008. They were staring down NFL history.

The Patriots came into the game with a perfect 18–0 record. The 1972 Miami Dolphins were the only perfect Super Bowl champion, finishing 17–0. New England had a chance to become the first NFL team to finish a season 19–0.

The surprising Giants had lost six games, including one to the Patriots. During the playoffs, however, they got on a roll. New York won three road games, including an overtime victory at Green Bay in the NFC Championship Game, to reach the Super Bowl.

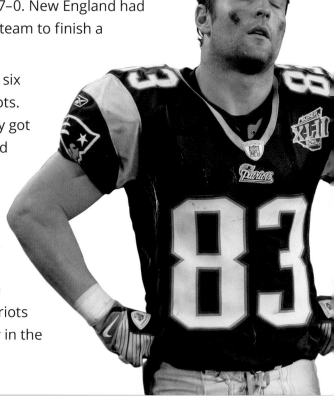

Even though both teams had high-powered offenses, the game was a defensive struggle. The Patriots led 7–3 after three quarters. Early in the

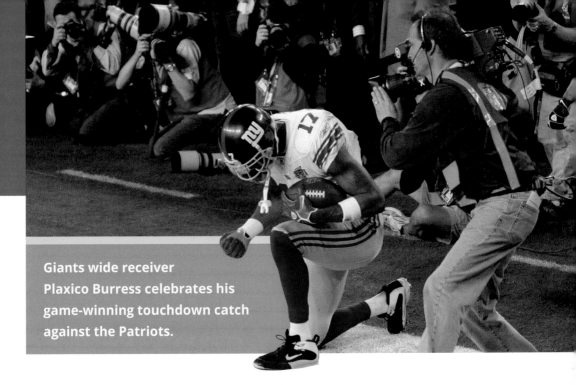

Giants wide receiver Plaxico Burress celebrates his game-winning touchdown catch against the Patriots.

fourth quarter, Giants quarterback Eli Manning threw a touchdown pass to backup wide receiver David Tyree to give them a 10–7 lead.

New England's perfect season was in jeopardy. But Brady came to the rescue. He threw a 6-yard touchdown pass to Randy Moss with 2:42 to play. The Patriots led 14–10 and needed one more defensive stop to close out the perfect season.

With about a minute to play, the Patriots had history—and Manning—in their grasp. New England's defense was close to sacking the Giants quarterback on a crucial third-down play near midfield. Manning shook free, however, and heaved the ball down the field. Tyree was standing at the New England 25, where he and safety Rodney Harrison went up for the ball. Tyree got his hands on it, then pinned it to his helmet as Harrison brought him down.

Tyree's catch kept the drive alive for the Giants. Moments later, Manning threw a 13-yard touchdown pass to Plaxico Burress. New York won 17–14, and New England had to settle for 18–1.

3

Joe Namath stood tall in the Jets' Super Bowl upset of the Baltimore Colts.

Namath Calls His Shot

In the lead-up to Super Bowl III in Miami, hardly anyone gave the underdog New York Jets a chance.

At the time, pro football was split into two leagues. The American Football League (AFL) started in 1960 as a rival to the NFL. In 1966 the leagues decided to merge, with each league's champion meeting at the end of the season in the Super Bowl.

The NFL was the dominant league, and the Green Bay Packers proved it by crushing the AFL champs in the first two Super Bowls. This time, it was supposed to be the Baltimore Colts' turn to hammer the AFL's Jets. The Colts had gone 13–1 with a punishing defense that allowed just over 10 points per game.

But quarterback Joe Namath wasn't intimidated. His Jets had gone 11–3 in the AFL, a league he knew was good and getting better every year. He told everybody he thought his team could win the game. Three nights before the game, he yelled to a fan that he guaranteed a Jets victory.

The 25-year-old quarterback had a lot of confidence. He became a legend when he backed it up. Namath and the Jets offense weren't dominant, but they found ways to get down the field and put points on the board. A touchdown run by Matt Snell and three field goals gave New York a 16–0 lead after three quarters.

The Jets defense was great, too. They intercepted four passes and forced five Colts turnovers. Baltimore didn't score until three minutes left in the game. By then, it was too late.

Namath had led the Jets to an unlikely 16–7 victory. This was more than just a win for the Jets, though. This was a win for the AFL, which was constantly fighting for respect. A year later, the two leagues joined forces to become the NFL we know today.

2

Fans braved subzero temperatures all day as they watched the Packers and Cowboys battle in the Ice Bowl.

The Ice Bowl

Mother Nature played a starring role in the 1967 NFL Championship Game, held at Lambeau Field in Green Bay. The Packers and the visiting Dallas Cowboys squared off for the championship for the second year in a row. A year earlier, Green Bay had won in a shootout in relatively balmy weather in Dallas. Conditions were a bit different for this one.

The temperature was minus−13 degrees Fahrenheit (−25°C) at kickoff. It was the coldest game ever played, and it quickly became known as the "Ice Bowl." Players on both teams spent the day trying to stay warm. They also battled just to stay on their feet. The frozen turf caused players to slip and fall all day long.

Led by quarterback Bart Starr, the Packers jumped to an early lead. Starr threw two touchdown passes to Boyd Dowler to put Green Bay ahead 14–0. But Dallas slowly chipped away at the lead. The defense scored a touchdown. Then a field goal cut Green Bay's lead to 14–10

Officials signal a touchdown after Bart Starr, *15*, burrowed into the end zone in the game's final seconds.

END OF A DYNASTY

The Ice Bowl represented a turning point in Green Bay Packers history. It was the final Lambeau Field game for legendary coach Vince Lombardi, who retired at the end of the season. Two weeks later, the Packers whipped the Oakland Raiders 33–14 in Super Bowl II. But after winning five NFL titles in seven years, the Packers made the playoffs just twice in the next 25 years.

at halftime. In the fourth quarter, halfback Dan Reeves threw a 50-yard touchdown pass to Lance Rentzel. That gave the Cowboys their first lead, 17–14.

The Cowboys held on into the final, frigid seconds. Starr led a drive to the Dallas 1-yard line, but only 16 seconds remained. The slippery field made running difficult. Starr took a chance anyway. He took the snap and stepped to his right. Packers guard Jerry Kramer and center Ken Bowman pushed Cowboys defensive tackle Jethro Pugh back into the end zone, and Starr fell across the goal line for the touchdown and a 21–17 victory.

1

Giants halfback Frank Gifford tries to outrun a Colts defender in the 1958 NFL Championship Game.

Sudden-Death Thriller

Some games are considered great because they're close and exciting. Some earn the label for the legendary players taking key roles in the spotlight. And some games are remembered for the impact they have on their sport. The 1958 NFL Championship Game had all that and more.

In 1958 professional football was not the massively popular game that it is today. Before 1958 it was rare to see an NFL game on national television. Some games weren't even televised locally. Now every game is on television, and TV networks cover the NFL 365 days a year.

But it wasn't just TV. The world of pro football was much smaller in 1958. The AFL didn't yet exist. The first

24

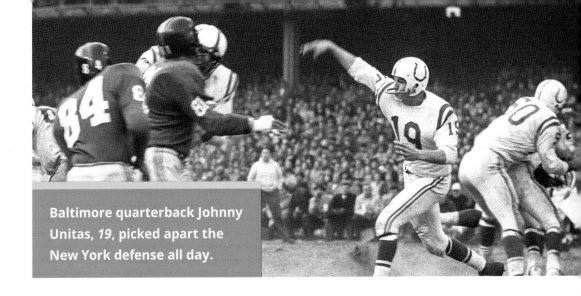

Baltimore quarterback Johnny Unitas, *19*, picked apart the New York defense all day.

Super Bowl was still eight years away. The NFL had just 12 teams that were divided into two divisions. The division winners met in the NFL Championship Game.

That's when the New York Giants and Baltimore Colts helped take the NFL to a new level. NBC-TV televised the game, making it available to viewers from coast to coast. And those who tuned in got to watch one of the greatest games in sports history.

The Colts were led by Johnny Unitas. He was only 25 years old but was already a two-time Pro Bowl quarterback. Meanwhile, nobody for the Giants shone more brightly than halfback Frank Gifford. The dual-threat star was the 1956 NFL Most Valuable Player and a six-time Pro Bowler.

Both legends played key roles on this day, though for different reasons. Unitas threw for 349 yards, and Baltimore took advantage of two Gifford fumbles to post a 14–3 halftime lead. But the Giants fought back. First the New York defense stood its ground, denying the Colts on a goal-line stand in the third quarter. Then the offense began to click.

From his own 13-yard line, Giants quarterback Charlie Conerly connected with receiver Kyle Rote over the middle, and Rote rambled to the Colts 25. Rote fumbled when he was brought down, but teammate

Alex Webster picked up the ball and advanced it to the Baltimore 1. Two plays later, Mel Triplett barreled into the end zone, and the Giants were back in it.

On their next drive, the Giants marched 81 yards to take the lead. Gifford caught a 15-yard touchdown pass from Conerly early in the fourth quarter to put New York on top 17–14.

The defenses dominated the rest of the quarter until the Colts got the ball back for one last chance. Taking over at his own 14-yard line, Unitas hit Raymond Berry on three straight passes for 62 total yards. As time was running out, Baltimore's Steve Myhra made a 20-yard field goal to tie the game 17–17.

In those days, NFL rules allowed for tie games during the regular season. No postseason game had yet been tied after 60 minutes. Thus, the national television audience was about to watch the NFL's first sudden-death overtime game.

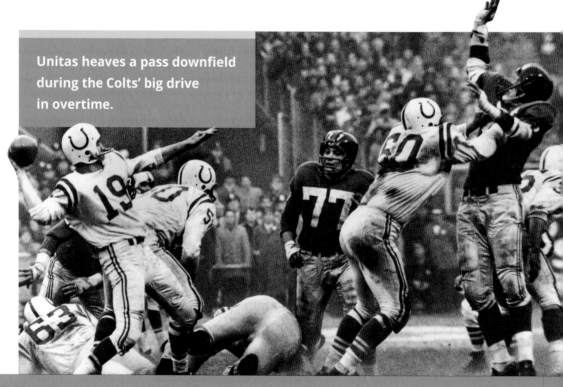

Unitas heaves a pass downfield during the Colts' big drive in overtime.

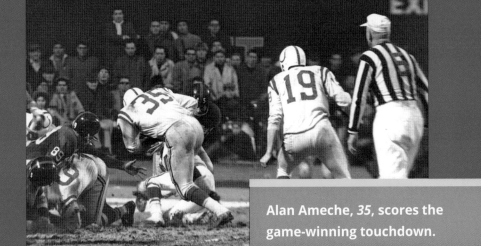

Alan Ameche, *35*, scores the game-winning touchdown.

CALL TO THE HALL

The 1958 NFL Championship Game featured 17 players or coaches who were later inducted into the Pro Football Hall of Fame. Each team had six players, including such legends as Unitas, Berry, Lenny Moore, Sam Huff, Gifford, and Emlen Tunnell. Two Giants assistant coaches went on to Hall of Fame careers with other teams—Tom Landry (Dallas Cowboys) and Vince Lombardi (Green Bay Packers).

The Giants won the coin toss but couldn't move the ball. After a punt, Unitas took over. He connected again with Berry on a 21-yard pass for a first down. Then he called an audible that sprung running back Alan Ameche for a 23-yard gain. With the ball at the 1-yard line, Ameche got the ball again and plunged across the goal line for the game-winning touchdown.

Pro football would never be the same. Spurred by the attention the game drew across the country, eight ownership groups spent the next year forming a new league. The AFL began play in 1960. That led to a merger with the NFL, the Super Bowl, and national television deals that nobody could have imagined just a few years earlier.

Honorable Mentions

CHARGERS 41, DOLPHINS 38: The San Diego Chargers jumped to a 24–0 lead after one quarter of this 1981 AFC playoff game. But Miami stormed back and actually led 38–31 in the fourth quarter before San Diego rallied for the overtime victory.

BILLS 41, OILERS 38: The Buffalo Bills pulled off the biggest comeback win in playoff history in this 1992 AFC wild card game. The Houston Oilers took a 35–3 lead before the Bills scored 35 points in a row. The Oilers tied it with a field goal, but the Bills won in overtime.

STEELERS 13, RAIDERS 7: The Oakland Raiders were moments away from a 7–6 victory in the 1972 AFC playoffs. Then Pittsburgh's Franco Harris caught a deflected pass and raced for a controversial touchdown. The catch became known as the "Immaculate Reception."

GIANTS 20, BILLS 19: With eight seconds left in Super Bowl XXV, the Bills had a chance to win their first championship. But kicker Scott Norwood's 47-yard field goal was wide right. The New York Giants survived to win the title.

EAGLES 38, GIANTS 31: Dubbed "Miracle at the New Meadowlands," the Giants led 31–10 with eight minutes to play in their December 2010 clash. But Philadelphia scored 21 straight points to tie the game. The Giants then failed to run out the clock, and on the last play they punted to DeSean Jackson, who returned it 65 yards for the game-winning touchdown.

RAIDERS 43, JETS 32: Known as the "Heidi Game," two of the AFL's top teams were playing on national TV in November 1968. The Jets led 32–29 with just over a minute to play when NBC-TV left the telecast at 7:00 p.m. Eastern time to run a regularly scheduled episode of a children's program called *Heidi*. After the switch, the Raiders scored two touchdowns in nine seconds to win the game, but a large portion of the audience was unable to watch the finish.

CHIEFS 31, BRONCOS 28: An epic duel between two of greatest quarterbacks of all time, the Broncos' John Elway and the Chiefs' Joe Montana, played out on Monday Night Football in October 1994. Both were the masters of late-game comebacks. Elway led the Broncos to a go-ahead touchdown with 1:30 to go. Montana then drove the Chiefs to the game-winning touchdown with eight seconds to go.

Glossary

audible

When the quarterback changes the play at the line of scrimmage after seeing how the defense has lined up.

balmy

Warm and comfortable.

dual threat

Very good at two different skills, such as running and receiving.

dynasty

A team that has an extended period of success, usually winning multiple championships in the process.

interception

A pass that is caught by the defense, instead of by the receiver to whom the quarterback was throwing.

legendary

Regarded as one of the best to ever play.

merge

Join with another to create something new, such as a company, a team, or a league.

overtime

The extra time needed to decide a game that is tied at the end of regulation.

playoffs

An annual tournament to determine the league champion.

sudden-death overtime

An extra period played to decide a tied game in which the first team to score is the winner.

For More Information

Books

Costas, Bob, and Joe Garner. *100 Yards of Glory: The Greatest Moments in NFL History*. Boston: Houghton Mifflin Harcourt, 2011.

Kovacs, Vic. *Touchdown! The History of Football*. New York: Crabtree Publishing Company, 2016.

Sports Illustrated. *Super Bowl Gold: 50 Years of the Big Game*. New York: Sports Illustrated Books, 2015.

Websites

To learn more about the NFL, visit **abdobooklinks.com**. These links are routinely monitored and updated to provide the most current information available.

Place to Visit

Pro Football Hall of Fame
2121 George Halas Drive NW
Canton, Ohio 44708
330-456-8207
www.profootballhof.com

The Hall of Fame is like a museum dedicated to football. There are exhibits on the origins of the game, artifacts from famous moments, and busts honoring the greatest players and coaches ever.

Index

About the Author

Brian Howell is a freelance writer based in Denver, Colorado. He has been a sports journalist for more than 20 years and has written dozens of books about sports and two about American history. A native of Colorado, he lives with his wife and four children in his home state.